He is Coming

By Jerome Miller AKA Transpernt Thought

© Jerome Miller

Jerome Miller
2955 Central Park Dr
Sierra Vista AZ 85635
www.example.com

Prologue

He is coming is a book to introduce the world to a writer that's been right in front of you this whole time. This book is just the beginning as it's purpose is to start the journey into Transparent Thought. Then I'll show you the Medicine for my pain. I truly hope you enjoy the words you find on these pages but more than that. I hope these words reach the people and that it speaks to their situation and their souls.
                              -Transpernt Thought

Thank you first and foremost to My lord and savior above Thank you to my Goodfellas who supported me from day one and to My Hawaii Ohana who showed me love in moments I thought I was alone. Thank you to Kody, Josh and Makayla for just supporting a strangers dreams. Thanks to Ciara and Brandon for being my left and right to help me fight my own bull shit. Thanks to CJack and shadow Designs for this fire ass cover. Thank you Eric just being the constant example for your lil bro. Thank you Samanda for breathing life into a lost soul. Thank you Natalie for being the Shehulk and motivating me to reach for the stars. And thank you Eric and Mavis Miller for giving me life and just constantly supporting me. Last but certainly not least thank you to my God given gift. My life coach, my soul, the wind beneath my wings, My constant reality check my best friend, my Muse, Chazney Alexandria Spears. Thank you for rocking with me for 16 or 17 plus years. Thank you to everyone and anybody whose been with me since day one yes that means you too Kev and Kimi

He is coming

He was born in the stone of the city of the rose. He was the seed that was never supposed to have rose. He is the seed of a Queen and Chosen King. He is the one whose name shall ring. Ring to glory I say wait til you hear his story I say!!! He has hidden himself from the light not because he fears it but because his light shines brighter than the sun. Success has knocked on his door many of times and he has run. As quick as the wind as fast as a bullet out this worlds gun. He has sat and watch from the shadows. He has sat back and purposely and gracefully lost battles Why you ask? So others could feel empowered so others could live and grow from his light. Don't be fooled fool he is not God but from the mold. He is cut from the cloth of old. He has sat back for many a year and shed a many a tear. However something has spoken to him some spirit has spoken in his ear this year. His eyes are open and his heart beats differently cuz no more is he feeding his light to those who wish him ill. In this year he has awaken like a slumbering giant no longer reliant. He is no longer reliant. He is no longer reliant I said!!! On you or them he is only relying on him. He has decided it is now time for him to come. It is now time for him to rise up from his mental slums. He has decided that it is time no passed time for his time and his bell has rung. It is time for his battles to be won. Get ready for all those who ignored him for all those who forgot to adore him. For all those who deemed him ununique. Get ready as he stands to his feet. Do you hear him running cuz hear he come a running. Here the thunder roar in him and feel the heat from the flames burning deep in his soul. Are you ready. Cuz I know you ain't prepared. Are you scared. Don't fear. But be aware He...Is....Coming!!!

HE

He is you and he is me. He is waiting on you and me. He needs to stand. He can be a she or whatever he wants to be in a world of iniquity and calamity he can be what he or she chooses to be. He needs to stand and rise up against the evil holding the world and which he lives in hostage. The world he lives in voted a man dumber than a sausage as its leader. He has swallowed enough of his own tears. I believe you can count the millions by liters. He has dreams. However the world has held him in contempt how dare he dream. How dare he dream of a world where people are allowed to speak freely while respecting those who think differently gracefully and peacefully. How dare he dream of actually having goals and ambition passed washing dishes. How dare he chose to dream of a world with a justice system that leaves him feeling safe not feeling no one cares so fuck it it's just us. How dare he. Cuz he is we and we is he. So how dare we want a systematic system that systematically benefits more than just them or just him but all. Cuz shouldn't we all be allowed to receive the call of liberty. Or is justice for all just a lie setting he up for a great fall. How dare he want a world where boys and girls are mentored by responsible responding parents. Not moral-less pop stars with no ethical sense apparent. He is sorry he wants to live in a world where it's safe to live transparent. He apologizes for speaking his truth. He just wishes he lived in a world that didn't wanna put his neck in a nuse. He is sorry for his rambling but remember he is me and me is you. If we want a better world we need to come together and do what we need to do.

Transparent Mindset

Transparent thought it's so clear you might see past the point. you ain't ready. To understand my mindset. yours ain't ready but I'm about to mamba this mentality. Let's rumble I swear I win in any reality. I didn't come to play. Cuz I'll just show up with the truth and you'll exit stage left. I've set by long enough I'm coming off the shelf. I've watched and the world ain't ready but I'm coming transparently and apparently my mindset is that I'm not just coming I'm nuttin to mess with. My words about to bring life and it's about turn on the light. So just make sure your ready cuz I'm comin to rise in the mornin and take over the night with my transparent mindset.

Living in Color

We met in a world not created for us. We walk through the sands and they still ain't give us our land. Some of us have fallen. Some to the world some to the cops in a hotel room. Now I'm sitting here like I'm in Marvin room. Because they all look like strangers. My melanin brings so many dangers. I just wish they could see the strength. Keep shooting us down because nothing you do is going change or lessen the strength in us.

Ghost

These ghost keep calling… on my knees I keep falling. This silence is so loud. The ghost of your memory crowding me. These walls keep telling our story.

Your voicemails keep saying you're sorry. These ghost keep calling me to come back but I can't. I need to be free. I need to do this for me. There is still so much rebuilding. These damn ghost keep calling. But know more so no more falling. I must stand. It's myself I know I need to find. It's me that I need to find. I got lost in we. These ghost are calling but I'm not answering.........

Exploration
Lay down let me interrupt your mind. Let me insert my thought into your enteral spirit. Let's flow down your river of thought. Let me hold your physical as I explore your mental. Let me get deep in to your psyche. Turn over and let me plug into you emotional canal. Let me eat from your Milky Way. Let me pick you up and take you on a trip. Get on your knees and worship the life creator. Walk with me and rise to the next level on our

love elevator. Let me bring elation. Let me be the master of your incantation. Let us go to a place of euphoric proportions. Let our life force combine to find our joint revelations. Then let our lands lie together and let the ocean crash on our shores. Let me show you I'm yours and you're mine and that we have bonded and now walk with one mind.

Early morning thoughts
Driving down this life like a one way the wrong way. Like I'm trying to get to the runway to run away. I'm tied down so I gotta stay. I don't know why I'm running. Cuz no matter what I do life is coming. A strong wall can crumble. A weak heart going to always

mumble. The lost will always stumble. You making losing moves in these streets. You lost yourself you don't even recognize your own heartbeat. You showing weakness while you trying to hide your weakness. You played the game. You knew you was gon lose. You got some choices but you'll never choose.

Elected
Truly blessed they can't stop me. They lucky I've been so quiet but time to make this noise. No longer silent so you can be silent about the things I elected you to speak on. You got the votes. Now you in Washington voting to cut your constituents Throat. You get elected. Then……………..Nothing

Where has he gone

Where has he gone where is his smile where is his passion, his drive, and his will ever lasting. where are his dreams where is the fire that once burned inside like a volcano ready to bust at the seams. He seems to be gone from this world but lost to this world because where is he now. where is the man he was to become. where is the family he was to have and the fame he imagined as a boy. where is he? If he is still there can he see me? Can he see the pain? can he feel the depression that plagues my heart and my brain? is he up late nights watching me toss and turn as I sit back and let precious moments and opportunities burn. I wonder does he sit back and shake his head and wonder if I'll ever learn? where has he gone when will he return? does he sit back and wonder if his lord has stricken him from the favored list . He must lust to return to claim his true voice. Does he once again get a chance at being favored once again and fully pardoned of all his sins? does he want a new genesis or does he just want a revelation? I wonder which will gain his true elation. he gotta be sure his lord runs low on patience. Where has he gone? Will he ever return? will I ever gain the respect he lived to earn? i miss him I cry for him. I look in the mirror and he is not there but there only in memory. I die in this world or do I even exist because he is me and I am gone. so.....where...has....he....gone

Ripple Effect

I moving different sense I met you. You got me not thinking right but I'm ok with being wrong. Like Trey songs let's be disrespectful. Girl i ain't just trying to drink from your cup I'm trying to fill it up. You got me opening my eyes looking for you. You got me feeling like we could embark on something true. Got me dreaming when I know I'm awake. Dreams come and go but I swear I'm ok with never being awake. You came and skipped your rock against my lake. Cuz I'm starting to feel the ripple effect. And I know you got that piece of paper but it ain't my fault he forgot and got you feeling neglect. Not my fault he got you feeling like an option and not the queen elect.

You ain't even gotta ask outta a million you'll always be the one I'll select.

Grab your binoculars

I see you watching. Go run get your binoculars. You mutha fuckers just a bunch of stalkers. Dead soul snatchers. I see you watching and waiting for the fall. The fall ain't coming fuck all y'all. I see you with your binoculars. Make sure you're looking closely. Cuz I'm moving too much so you might lose me. I know I did but I've found him. He said he's coming back and he about to shock the world. Lock it up boys and girls. Grab your binoculars so you can watch the fire works. Grab your binoculars cuz your distraction, situation and drama didn't work. He says he knows his worth. He said grab your binoculars cuz things about to get sticky like he jacked off mrs. buttersworth. You bitches tried to play me like you were Diddy and I was Fonsworth. You try to sell me out like I was the garden. Now grab your binoculars and watch me grow. The seed has been planted and he has landed better yet he has risen. Cuz this lame ass life that you once convinced him to live is done. So grab your binoculars son. Cuz understand he is me and his worth is mine and I now understand I was put here to shine

Questions
When is it enough? When can I lay down my head. When can I smell the

air? When is it my time? When will I be allowed to shine? I've played the game by your rules. When do I find my truth? Who can I trust? Where is the love of my life. Who keeps my heart safe at night? Why do I keep going. When life's bullshit is constantly snowing on me. Why do I try so hard to invest in positivity. When it stay eluding me. When will someone choose me? When will someone value and never want to lose me?Just when, why, where and how am I supposed to keep going? Cuz daily I just feel like dying. I guess I'm just tired of trying.

Momma
Momma you brought me in this world. I hope you know you're my world. You're always my light when I'm fall in that dark place. I thank God for your

grace. I can't imagine life without that smile upon your face. I've seen you cry and every time I just wanted the cause to die. You are more than my rock. You are my mountain. You are more than my air. You are my soul. You're more than my protector. You're my safe place. I love you endlessly. You are the reason there is any good in me. My spirit Cries for you daily. Without you I'd go crazy. You are my starting point and you are where my mind ends every night. Momma you are my love. You are my gift bestowed upon me from above. You brought me in this world naked. Until this day you still see me naked. You love me through my flaws. You love me through my pain. You love me through my rain. I just thank God for my momma.

No directions

Listen we ain't shit. This shit got me going! This shit falling like it's snowing. Where we going? We riding with no destination. We fucking with no elation. You winning but hold your celebration. We in love , we done, we together again. I'm tired of the frustration. But I need you. You want me. We poison. Being with you is my prison. I can't leave. But my sleeve wet from these tears. We've been trying for years. Where we going. Got me on my knees looking for directions but God was never the GPS for this trip. But all these feelings go away when I taste those strawberry lips. I guess there's no end to these frivolous trips.

Time and Life

Where does time go. I think time is an illusion. I think it in cahoots with life. I think it's collusion. I think they both plan to stress me. Cuz where does time go and what did I do with it to further my life. Time moves but life stays stagnant. Like a rat on a wheel it's blatant. It's like time and life have created a system. Don't get me wrong I'm not blaming them. I'm just stating the obviously not obvious. It's like a game and they teamed up to win. It's only when we openly understand this that we begin to win. Time and life take so much but there's a way to regain what has been taken. We live life in fear. However if we embraced the fears in life then we stop waisting time and begin moving. It's crazy because life is the opponent but yet the teacher but we have to take the time to think before we react. Through life we allow our emotions to react to life. Instead allowing of seeing how much time we waste being overly emotional to life. Time and life will not stop moving while being led by our emotions keeps us sitting still. What would happen if we allowed life's lessons to lead our emotions instead allowing our emotions to lead our life lessons. How much time would we save. That's all I got cuz I know time is ticking on this life just thought I'd point it out before I see the grave.

The fight within part 1
I got nothing to write. Just turn off the light. My mind is blocked. I know you're shocked. Nah delete that line. Jerome what you thinking you'll never shine. Where's are those great words? Nobody wants to read your pain.

Nobody cares that tears fall from your eyes like rain. Why won't the ideas flow to me. The same reason love will never come to me. Why can't I drift away? Why can't I go to that place? That place I go to be great. Nothing to write but I know I got plenty to say. Man just quit nobody wants you to hear what you have to say. My mind is heavy. No that's not what you wanna say. What am I feeling? Lord!!!! Break me down and rebuild me. There's no more fruit on my tree. Can't sleep. Up late night afraid to die. Afraid this night will be the never ending night. Sitting here wondering if there's anything left. I gotta get this book done. For once I wanna be the favorite son. You're not making sense. I haven't been happy since..... nah let's not talk about that. My procrastination will be my only legacy. My deepest fear is that I'll die and no one will cry for or even remember me. I hope I can change the world. You can't even save your Niece's world. You've failed those girls. None of your soldiers love you. They don't miss you. They don't need you. You're lost and don't know what to do. Just walk away. Listen and give in to what the critics say. Just let go......

Think of me
Breathe. Think of us together. Think of me when you feel like you're falling. Think of me when you need a pick me up. Think of me when you feel you need to fill your cup up. I'll never let you fall. Unless its for me. Just breathe. Think of my heartbeat. Cuz I think of you with every heartbeat. No anxiety. Cuz it's me and you against society. Just think of me.

Just telling the truth

Listen I'm here do you see me or do you see my movement. Y'all burning Nike but y'all still fail to se me. Y'all hoping for my fall but mad I had to take a knee and take a breath from the air. constantly being driven out of one chosen race. Not chosen to live but chosen to be ridiculed and eradicated. Chosen to be taught and endorsed for self hate. Chosen never early but always late. Chosen to sleep but. Chosen to be feared if I awake from my Jim Crow nap. You checking my silent conversation while your leader of the not free world freely trades American values. Why the value of my rights don't add up to your social views? Who needs a space force when Facebook is the new frontier? It's the new battle ground. So many Facebook soldiers. Yelling support the troops but you would never sign up. Oops. I'm not supposed to say that cuz I'm not supposed to tell your secret. My soldierly sacrifice is to support you bottom line. The bottom line is you just using the troops as a distraction to this one fact. Cops commit a crime, your elected officials say obscene and disrespectful things and not a sound but you make more then a sound about my silence.

Dirty

Let me just get straight to business. I shouldve just minded my business. You Wall Street talkers. Who look like street walkers about to make me just kill this. I was just trying to get to a nice place. I was just trying to put a smile on your face. Meanwhile you was taking liberties behind my face. You were just planting seed to destroy my place. Now once again we getting down to business so maybe you deserve the profit for trying to destroy this prophet. I was sent here from God I got distracted for a bit but now I'm back on my job no I don't mean head cuz that's your business cuz I swear you muthafuckers are like cock blocks you'll never let me get ahead. You rather see me dead. Or would you rather turn me into you instead? Nevermind I can't get my mind to be so empty thats ok stay messy and I'll just stay busy getting mine. Cuz god is about to bless me. What you mad cuz I'm black happy and I had to wait my turn in this world's line. No not the line in your nose but that one line that's ready to shine.

I'm Here

You've been distracted by the illusion. You never stopped to see me. I've been sitting in the darkness. Waiting to strike. You thought I was just a slave for your likes. I'm so much more. Now I'm ready now I'm walking through the door now im coming. Now I'm here. Now open your ears. Now you all will feel the pain behind these silent tears. Prepare your self for the real me cuz I have landed. I'm hear for the hearts and minds that feel stranded. I'm hear to open the gate with my key words. I'm here no longer to be silent but to be heard

About the Author

Jerome Miller AKA. Transpernt Thought. Is from Tyler Texas he is the Son of Mavis and Eric Miller Sr. Jerome was born in 1984 but Transpernt Thought was born when Jerome was just 14 years old when he started writing. Transpernt Thought or Jerome which ever you decide to call me. Has one goal and that's to bring light to not just his darkness but to the darkness that plagues the world.

Made in the USA
Middletown, DE
24 December 2022

20328631R00018